AF445737

The British Claim

The most punctual passage by Europeans upon the Indian Ocean was by the Portuguese sailor Bartholomew Dias, who adjusted the Cape of Storms (later the Cape of Good Hope) in 1488. He wandered no farther than the juncture of the Atlantic and Indian Oceans, and it would not be for one more decade that his comrade Vasco da Gama squeezed his revelations further east to the bank of India. The Portuguese then established a presence on the east coast of Africa, and with the entire Orient to themselves, undertook numerous voyages of exploration, not all of which were directly recorded. There is, consequently, a way of thinking upholding the idea that it was the Portuguese who were the main Europeans to look at the incredible southern land. Supporting this hypothesis are antiquated Portuguese guides of a coast that likely could be Australia, and intermittent relics of Portuguese beginning that have been found in different spots in Australia.

Perhaps the most convincing contention for earlier Portuguese disclosure is rationale. The Portuguese set up settlements in India and different focuses in Southeast Asia, with Portuguese Timor a simple 400 miles from the Australian coast. Remembering the extent of Portuguese sea investigation, there is no explanation by any means to expect that the Portuguese would not have followed the regular movement of the Malay Archipelago to show up definitively on the north shore of Terra Australis. This would unquestionably be in character, and as early Portuguese sailors traveled the Malay Archipelago, it appears to be practically inescapable that they would have found Australia. They could scarcely have considered what it was, yet it would in any case have given them earlier claim.

Nonetheless, eventually, it was Dutch sailor Willem Janszoon, on board the Dutch East India Company vessel Duyfken, who asserted those shrubs. It is currently an acknowledged reality that his undertaking was quick to contact the shores of what might today be the northern tip of Queensland.

Janszoon was followed very soon subsequently by a Spanish endeavor drove by Portuguese pilot Pedro Fernandes de Queirós. This little armada showed up from the east, having made various more modest disclosures on the way around Cape Horn. Queirós indeed erroneously took the New Hebrides to be the much-celebrated southern landmass, so he named it Austrialia del Espiritu Santo, or the Southern Land of the Holy Spirit, out of appreciation for the Spanish queen

Margaret of Austria. The close to suggest the skyline was a subordinate commander of Queirós named Luís Vaz de Torres, who cruised in from the east in July 1606. Adhering toward the south shore of Papua, New Guinea, he went through Torres Strait, which was in this manner named after him. He stopped momentarily on the northern tip of Cape York prior to forging ahead through the Malay Archipelago.

For the rest of the seventeenth century, incessant Dutch visits would be made to the shore of this immense and confounding area, and gratitude to this it was ostensibly asserted by the Dutch, who called it New Holland. They were not arranged to settle and colonize, in any case; the Dutch were principally a commercial group, and their targets were gold, flavors, slaves, and intermittent Christian teacher work. The bank of Australia seemed to not have anything of direct revenue to these Dutch sailors, which guaranteed they moved on.

Thus, by the 1700s, the presence of the Terra Australis was by and large known and comprehended, and steadily, its shores were noticed and planned. All things considered, the southern coast would not be planned exhaustively until the nineteenth century, however Van Diemen's Land, an island off the south coast currently called Tasmania, was recognized in 1642 by Dutch sailor Abel Tasman.
A couple of months after the fact, this gutsy Dutchman would add New Zealand to the guide of the known world.

The English were the best maritime power in Europe, yet they showed up on the scene rather later. The first to seem was William Dampier, commander of the HMS Roebuck, in 1699, later he had been allowed a Royal Commission by King William III to investigate the east shoreline of New Holland. By then, the general global balance of power was shifting, and with the English gaining a solid foothold in India, their supremacy in the Indian Ocean trade zone began. The Dutch, once overwhelming in the district, started gradually to lose ground, getting out of dispute as a significant worldwide exchanging power. So too were the Portuguese, likewise once predominant in the area. It was presently the French and the English who were confronting each other down in a mission to overwhelm the world, yet their majestic advantages were centered basically in India and the East Indies, just as the Caribbean and the Americas. Subsequently, the capability of a huge, for all intents and purposes uninhabited incredible southern landmass didn't hold much interest.

Between the 1699 undertaking of William Dampier and the 1770 campaign of the HMS Endeavor, minimal European traffic upset the epochal sleep of Australia. Be that as it may, times were evolving. As the Endeavor gauged anchor and got out of Botany Bay, Marie-Antoinette was pledged to King

Louis XVI of France, and the French Revolution was not too far off. In the United Kingdom itself, the Catholic King James II of England had been ousted by an alliance of Parliamentarians and the Protestant William of Orange, which set off a financial and capital restoration in England, the establishing of the Bank of England, and a gigantic augmentation of the interests and impact of the strong British East India Company.

By then the world was largely mapped, with just regions such as the Arctic Archipelago and the two poles remaining terra incognita. A couple of holes should have been filled in to a great extent, however every one of the fundamental subtleties were known. Simultaneously, a lot of royal energy was influencing everything in Europe, especially in Britain. England remained at the cusp of worldwide strength thanks

as a rule to the Royal Navy, which arose in the seventeenth and eighteenth hundreds of years as a foundation fundamentally more than the amount of its parts. With huge resources accessible even in peacetime, endeavors of science and investigations were dispatched toward each path. This was done not exclusively to guarantee responsibility for field of worldwide investigation, yet additionally to undermine the magnificent desires of others, specifically the French.

In 1767, the Royal Society persuaded King George III to allocate funds for it to send an astronomer to the Pacific, and on January 1, 1768, the London Annual Register reported, "Mr. Banks, Dr. Solander, and Mr. Green the astronomer, set out for Deal, to embark on board the Endeavour, Captain Cook, for the South Seas, under the direction of the royal society, to observe the transit of Venus next summer, and to make discoveries." Mr. Banks was Joseph Banks, a botanist, and he brought along Dr. Daniel Solander, a Swedish naturalist. Charles Green was at that time the assistant to Nevil Maskelyne, the Astronomer Royal. The expedition, which would leave later in 1768, would be captained by Cook, a war veteran who had recently fought in the French & Indian War against the French in North America.

King George III

Banks

Solander

What the article didn't specify was that the Admiralty was additionally wanting to find the celebrated Terra Australis Incognita, the unbelievable "obscure southern land." This came out later, when the London Gazetteer wrote about August 18, 1768, "The courteous fellows, who are to cruise in a couple of days for George's Land, the new found island in the Pacific sea, with a goal to notice the Transit of Venus, are in like manner, we are solidly educated, to endeavor some new disclosures in that huge obscure parcel, over the scope 40." As this proposes, the British definitely realized that there was a for the most part neglected landmass in the area, and this is on the grounds that Europeans had located the shore of Australia more than 150 years earlier.

When Captain James Cook's undertaking started in 1768, it included in excess of 80 men, comprising of 73 mariners and 12 individuals from the Royal Marines. Apparently, the undertaking should be for completely logical – and consequently quiet – purposes. The Endeavor left Plymouth on August 26, 1768, and Cook arrived at Matavai Bay, Tahiti, on April 13, 1769. The main job needing to be done, other than everyday endurance, was planning to notice the travel of Venus that would happen on June 3.

Having finished the logical tasks, the Endeavor next set forth looking for Terra Australis. In the wake of cruising for almost two months, the team acquired the prize of being just the second gathering of Europeans to at any point visit New Zealand. They showed up on October 6, 1769, and Cook

portrayed a nerve racking encounter when the men came aground:
"MONDAY, ninth October.
… I went shorewards with a Party of men in the Pinnace and yawl joined by
Mr. Banks and Dr. Solander. We landed side by side of the Ship and on the
East side of the River recently referenced; yet seeing a portion of the Natives
on the opposite side of the River of whom I was envious of talking with, and
observing that we were unable to passage the River, I order'd the yawl in to
convey us over, and the pinnace to lay at the Entrance. Meanwhile the Indians
made off.
However we went the extent that their Hutts which lay around 2 or 300 Yards
from the water side, leaving 4 young men to deal with the Yawl, which we
had no sooner avoided than 4 Men accompanied regard to the forest on the
opposite side the River, and would positively have cut her off had not the
People in the Pinnace discover'd them and called to her to drop down the
Stream, which they did, being intently persued by the Indians. The coxswain
of the Pinnace, who had the charge of the Boats, seeing this, fir'd 2 Musquets
over their Heads; the principal made them pause and Look round them,
however the second they failed to acknowledge; whereupon a third was fir'd
and kill'd one of them upon the Spot similarly as he planned to dash his lance
at the Boat. At this the other 3 stood unmoving briefly, apparently very
astonished; pondering, almost certainly, what it was that had along these lines
kill'd their Comrade; yet when they recuperated themselves they made off,
hauling the Dead body a little way and afterward left it. Upon our hearing the
report of the Musquets we quickly repair'd to the Boats, and in the wake of
review the Dead body we return'd on board."

Over the next weeks, Cook dedicated himself to making an itemized guide
of the New Zealand coast. Cruising west, Cook wanted to arrive at Van
Diemen's Land, referred to now as Tasmania, yet all things considered, the
breezes constrained him north, driving him and his men toward the
southeastern bank of Australia. As destiny would have it, they were the main
Europeans to land around here. Cook recorded in his diary, "THURSDAY,
nineteenth. At 5, set the Topsails close reef'd, and 6, saw land stretching out
from North-East to West, distance 5 or 6 Leagues, having 80 spans, fine
sandy base. … The Southermost point of land we had in sight… I decided to
lay in the Latitude of 38 degrees 0 minutes South and in the Longitude of 211
degrees 7 minutes West from the Meridian of Greenwich. I have named it
Point Hicks, since Lieutenant Hicks was the

first who discover'd this Land. Toward the Southward of this point we could
see no land, but it was clear in that Quarter, and by our Longitude contrasted
and that of Tasman's, the assortment of Van Diemen's territory should have

bore due South from us, and from the before long falling of the Sea later the breeze lessened I had motivation to figure it did; Nonetheless as we didn't see it, and tracking down the Coast to drift North-East and South-West, or fairly more toward the Westward, makes me Doubtfull whether they are one land or no. However, every one who contrasts this Journal and that of Tasman's will be as great an appointed authority as I am; yet it is important to see that I don't take the Situation of Vandiemen's from the Printed Charts, yet from the concentrate of Tasman's Journal, distributed by Dirk Rembrantse. … What we have at this point seen of this land shows up rather low, and not uneven, the substance of the Country green and Woody, however the Sea shore is every one of the a white Sand."

Landing of Captain Cook at Botany Bay, 1770, by E. Phillips Fox (1902)

Cook next sailed the Endeavor north, exploring the coastline and making copious notes until he came upon a wide inlet, at which point the crew anchored and Cook and some of his men actually went ashore. Cook stated, "Sunday, sixth. In the evening the Yawl return'd from fishing, having Caught 2 Sting beams weighing close to 600 pounds. The extraordinary amount of plants Mr. Banks and Dr. Solander found here occasioned my giving it the Name of Botany Bay. It is arranged in the Latitude of 34 degrees 0 minutes South,

Longitude 208 degrees 37 minutes West. It is capacious, safe, and Commodious; it may be known by the land on the Sea Coast, which is of a pretty even and moderate height, Rather higher than it is inland, with steep rocky Clifts next the Sea, and looks like a long Island lying close under the Shore. … We Anchor'd near the South Shore about a Mile within the

Entrance for the Conveniency of Sailing with a Southerly wind and the getting of Fresh Water…. The Country is woody, low, and flat as far in as we could see, and I believe that the Soil is in general sandy. In the Wood are a variety of very beautiful birds, such as Cocatoos, Lorryquets, Parrots, etc., and crows Exactly like those we have in England. Water fowl is no less plenty about the head of the Harbour, where there is large flats of sand and Mud, on which they seek their food; the most of these were unknown to us, one sort especially, which was black and white, and as large as a Goose, but most like a Pelican. On the sand and Mud banks are Oysters, Muscles, Cockles, etc., which I believe are the Chief support of the inhabitants, who go into Shoald Water with their little Canoes and peck them out of the sand and Mud with their hands, and sometimes roast and Eat them in the Canoe, having often a fire for that purpose, as I suppose, for I know no other it can be for."

Cook additionally recorded his perceptions about the native individuals: "The Natives don't give off an impression of being various, neither do they appear to live in huge bodies, however dispers'd in little gatherings along by the Water side. Those I saw were comparably tall as Europeans, of an exceptionally dull earthy colored Color, yet not dark, nor had they wooly, frizled hair, however dark and slender like our own. No kind of Cloathing or Ornaments were at any point seen by any of us upon any of them, or in or about any of their Hutts; from which I reason that they never wear any. Some that we saw had their countenances and bodies painted with a kind of White Paint or Pigment. Altho' I have said that shell fish is their Chief help, yet they get different kinds of fish, some of which we observed simmering on the shoot whenever we first handled; a portion of these they hit with Gigs, and others they get with snare and line; we have seen them hit fish with gigs, and snares and lines are found in their Hutts. … However, we could know yet very little of their Customs, as we always were unable to frame any Connections with them; they had not really as touch'd the things we had left in their Hutts deliberately for them to remove. During our visit in this Harbor I made the English Colors be display'd aground each day, and an engraving to be removed upon one of the Trees close to the Watering place, presenting the Ship's Name, Date, etc."

A plaque commemorating Captain Cook's landing place

Cook's endeavor might have been for the reasons for science on a superficial level, yet when he asserted the new region, the British acknowledged it may fill in as a focal point of future British sea power and exchange the region.

In 1785, the French mounted a "logical" undertaking toward the South Pacific with the apparent motivation behind planning and investigation. On board were exactly 60 French convicts, plan, as per British undercover work sources, on setting up a maritime base on the shores of New Holland.

When insight about this arrived at the royal foundation in Britain, it was grasped by the unexpected criticalness to set up a British settlement before the French could arrive and do likewise. Driving the work to take functional ownership of New Holland was prominent British respectable man researcher and naturalist Joseph Banks, leader of the Royal Geographic Society and a significant figure in British investigation. Banks had went with Cook on his primer journey to New Holland, and he was by and large viewed in British circles as the main = expert on Australia. Having prior proclaimed the region ill suited for British colonization, he currently advocated colonization with an irate enAccordinglyiasm. Upheld by the Society and by the very compelling leading group of the British East India Company, the British foundation reacted rapidly. Thus, on May 13, 1787, the "Principal Fleet" set sail.

The armada of 11 boats was told by Captain Arthur Phillip, and a race with the French was on. It was not known exactly where the French armada was, however it was perceived, or maybe trusted, that the hurriedly collected British endeavor had the leap. To be protected, three of the quicker sends in the armada immediately split away, showing up in Botany Bay on January 18, 1788.

Phillip, a man of gigantic skill and incredibly chose sentiments, felt, following a couple of days, that Botany Bay didn't address the issues of a settlement, so he moved the whole armada a couple of miles north up the coast to Port Jackson.
The campaign made a stop in a shielded harbor, and the site was named Sydney Cove, presently pretty much the site of the Royal Botanical Gardens. The settlement that grew up around Port Jackson took on the name Sydney, to pay tribute to the British Home Secretary Lord Sydney.

Phillip

Greg O'Beirne's image of a sculpture of Phillip on the site

Meanwhile, the French armada showed up in Botany Bay barely behind the British, and as they did, Phillip dispatched a little power to Norfolk Island to guarantee that before the French could accumulate their faculties. The French waited for some time, however the deed was done, and New Holland, differentiated by normal understanding as the eastern shore of Terra Australis, was adequately British.

At least at first, this didn't change a lot. The British had made primer landfall on the Australian coast and set up an early settlement, however that scarcely made the way for sure fire predominance of the South Pacific. Regardless, it was a significant second in the majestic plots of the age, as history would later demonstrate. Actually, the British were currently in a situation to possibly extend power across the South Pacific to Spanish America, yet maybe above all, the British could now provoke the Spanish case toward the northwest shoreline of the American landmass. It likewise situated the British to challenge French and Dutch possessions in the Far East, and to more readily ensure British interests in India, which by then was arising as the virtual depository of the British Empire.

The British main story for all of this was the foundation of an abroad reformatory settlement, which tricked nobody. This story separated from the way that it

would at the appointed time become an unavoidable outcome, was pointed as much at resistance inside the United Kingdom with regards to the French or the Dutch. There was a lot of homegrown resistance to the foundation of a

British settlement in such a far off area, and one so detached from Europe at that. Chief Phillip was introduced as the principal Governor of the Colony, the province of New South Wales, which was officially settled on January 26, 1788. Before long thereafter, Phillip kept in touch with his support, Lord Shelburne, the ex-head of the state, that "it will be four years at any rate, before this Colony will actually want to help itself. In any case, My Lord, I feel that determination will answer each reason proposed by Government, and that this Country will henceforth be a most significant procurement to Great Britain from its circumstance." In the two cases, Governor Phillip would demonstrate right.

The British territorial claim on the east coast of New Holland comprised everything eastward of 135 degrees east, and all the islands of the Pacific Ocean between Cape York and the southern tip of Tasmania, then known as Van Diemen's Land. This included Norfolk Island and New Zealand.

The convict framework was the explanation that the province was established, and it was the explanation from there on why it was kept up with. No created country on Earth had a more extreme criminal code than the British around then. Convicts were moved from England to New South Wales in employed vehicle ships, shrunk by, among others, the British East India Company, and regularly conveyed in recommissioned slave ships shut of down by the abolition.
The organization of Camden, Calvert and King was additionally involved, and it was likely the biggest vehicle project worker of the period. The organization had initially been framed as a whaling armada, just to in this way progress into one that shipped slaves across the Atlantic and convicts to New South Wales.

Since the whole province was viewed as a jail, the jail hinders that were assembled were utilized uniquely as discipline for offenses submitted in the settlement. As a general rule, the jail populace was at freedom to work and live without limitation, however lashing was a standard discipline, and executions were extremely continuous. Without even a trace of a solid common organization, neighborhood systems could unquestionably be self-assertive and severe, and obviously convicts (particularly ladies) were powerless against maltreatment on account of the pilgrims to whom they were doled out. Those considered irredeemable even in the wake of being whipped and detained were shipped off the settlement of Norfolk Island, where
a more proper arrangement of imprisonment was set up, and where treatment of detainees was amazingly harsh.

Eventually, a settlement was established on Norfolk Island in 1788, principally to soothe tension on assets in Sydney. Phillip then sent various expeditions in search of somewhere with better soils, and in due course a site was identified at what is today the Sydney suburb of Parramatta. One more was set at Toongabbie. While challenges proceeded, under the energy of convict work, a conventional settlement before long started to come to fruition. Sydney Cove created as a port, yet the vast majority of the early populace moved inland and settled.

Development and Expansion

"The cenotaphs of species dead somewhere else, that in your cutoff points jump and swim and fly." – Bernard O'Dowd

The disclosure of a pragmatic course through the Blue Mountains put into high gear a whole shift of mentality both inside and outside of the developing state of New South Wales. From an intensive lack of engagement in movement to the province, other than for its fundamental managerial necessities, the British government started out of nowhere advancing migration, motioning in numerous ways the start of the finish of correctional transportation and the foundation of a more conventional British settlement. All of this would require some investment since the organization of the province was beset by time and distance, however after a short time, it was the foreigner boat that gradually started to supplant the convict transport as the most well-known sight in Port Jackson's harbor. The British press, presently better educated, started writing about the chances accessible in the new Australian province, where land awards were effectively realistic and where a man of unobtrusive capital could make a case for a real esatate surpassing the most well off assistants of England.

In 1818, the Home Secretary, first Viscount Sidmouth, tended to the House of Commons. In his discourse, he commented that the fear of transportation was currently a relic of times gone by, and that it had been prevailed by a typical craving for movement to that state that had once held such dread. This caused a circumstance by which the parcel of the shipped convict was considered less stunning, and episodes were recorded of British fighters positioned in Australia carrying out felonious violations to get the super durable right

of homestead in the new settlement, and a portion of the advantages offered on emancipists once they entered free life. Emancipists were, for sure, frequently ready to coordinate and carry on with altogether typical lives, profiting themselves of land assignments, entering the different parts of the organization, and occasionally showing up on the seat and the leader. Before the finish of Governor Lachlan Macquarie's term of office, in 1821, exactly 40,000 spirits lived in Sydney and the different satellite settlements of the state, and around 350,000 sections of land of land lay under occupation.

Viscount Sidmouth

Truth be told, the governorship of Major-General Lachlan Macquarie, somewhere in the range of 1810 and 1821, stamped something of an ocean change in such manner. His archetype, William Bligh, who was famous for being projected afloat during the uprising on the Bounty, carried his severe and solid disposition to the organization of the province. He acquired an arrangement of gubernatorial absolutism not at all like his Navy order, and of it he made very much like use. The separation from Britain, and the idea of the settlement in its initial years would in general legitimize this. The state was in pragmatic terms a jail with a shallow free organization, and Bligh and his archetypes had felt obliged to run the settlement in the way of jail governors.

Bligh

Macquarie, in any case, in spite of the fact that showing up in the province with comparative powers, was of a tendency to modernize and smooth out an extremely crude arrangement of the public authority of New South Wales.[1] It can't be said that he eliminated himself from overbearing and authoritarian acts of his archetypes, yet he is ordinarily viewed as the remainder of the dictators, and
William Bligh was unquestionably the most noticeably terrible of these.

Macquarie

Macquarie showed up with a contingent of the 73rd Regiment of Foot. Part of his command, and unquestionably the explanation that he showed up so intensely outfitted, was to handle and break down the New South Wales Corps. The NSWC, a wild assortment of equipped men, were raised at first to police the province, yet they were inclined to defilement, unrestrained, and absolutely hostile towards the organization. Some decommissioned individuals stayed in the state, and some were retained into the 73rd, yet most were localized back to England. Starting there onwards, until 1870, a unit of Imperial soldiers was pivoted in the settlement for the present, eliminating the job of guard from any privately comprised militia.

Macquarie, subsequently, represented with the equivalent general authority as his archetypes, yet under his term, the main conversation of the development of some kind of warning board as an antecedent to the foundation of a homegrown assembly was heard. The matter was put before the House of Commons in 1812, and it was concurred that such a chamber would be attractive, yet this was quickly overruled by the Secretary of State for the Colonies, the Earl of Bathurst, who was unwilling to think about a diminishment of the powers of his office for any nearby body. The power of Whitehall was practiced through his designated lead representative. Regardless, the matter was currently on the table, and definitely sooner or later it would be acted upon.

In the in the interim, Macquarie's term of office saw a lot of different developments, to be specific a survey of legal practice and a modification of the status and job of emancipists in the settlement who had by then filled impressively in number. There were inescapable social errors between free pilgrims and emancipists, maybe most intensely discernible in the inconsistent appropriation of land, still a methodology particularly in the possession of the lead representative. This cycle had until now would in general lean toward the "special features," or free settlers,
who numbered far less.[2] Correcting this awkwardness became one of Macquarie's vital targets. He noted, "When a convict has turned into a liberated individual, he ought to in all regards be considered on a balance with each and every man in the state, as indicated by his position throughout everyday life and character." This, in light of everything, was somewhat moderate, however it made him few very companions among the free pioneer community.

It is additionally fascinating to take note of that Macquarie's assumption on showing up in New South Wales was to experience a general public overwhelmed by the scrapings of
His Majesty's jail framework. He was, notwithstanding, generally shocked, and almost certainly delighted, to experience among the convicts and emancipists a large number of men of schooling, rearing, and character, specifically among the political detainees. Here he perceived a significant asset, and he set with regards to the errand of better incorporating these men

into pilgrim society.

This absolutely held out preferred possibilities of achievement over it may have assuming that he had attempted exactly the same thing in England. It was in the idea of the arising Australian person to shed the inflexible class shows of England, taking on rather a more libertarian arrangement of social chain of importance dependent on meritocracy rather than gentry, and without a doubt, the airs and graces of the British high societies were regularly not very much endured in the colony.

Despite this, and regardless of the lack of very capable men in the state, it required a lot of exertion and move to achieve what was a minor social unrest. Albeit not entirely effective, Macquarie endeavored to expand the organization, and eventually, his fundamental accomplishment was most likely to open the way for emancipists to serve in the legal executive, and on the seat. "I have volunteered to embrace another line of direct, imagining that liberation, when joined with integrity and since a long time ago attempted appropriate conduct, should lead a man back to that position in the public arena which he had relinquished, and do away, in to the extent the case will concede, with all hindsight of previous awful conduct."

These actually contained somewhat little advances, particularly thinking about that pioneers back in London actually didn't picture the state as anything over a jail camp. Unavoidably, in any case, the following period of regulatory advancement would be the foundation of some kind of protected government in the colony.

Macquarie may have been of a fairly more equitable outlook than his archetypes, yet he was as yet defenseless to subjective standard, bits of gossip about which intermittently appeared on the shores of Whitehall. The story is recounted a liberated individual who was whipped on Macquarie's orders with no fair treatment noticed, and when the man showed up back in England, scarified stripes and all, his story was accepted. As was standard, a commission of request was approved with a wide term of reference to inspect the laws and guidelines of the province, the utilizations of the settlement, the arrangement of government and the treatment of convicts, later which it was relied upon to make recommendations
for an overhaul.

The commission started its examination in 1819, staying in Sydney for a very long time. Macquarie's moves to put emancipists on the authoritative seat were not all around generally welcomed by the officials, and indeed, the lead representative himself was not especially praised in the last report. His term of office, notwithstanding, was regardless attracting to an end, and by 1824 he was dead.

His replacement, Major General Thomas Brisbane, would enter upon his term of office under intelligibly reconsidered terms of administration, and Brisbane would be the primary legislative head of New South Wales whose powers were restricted by resolution. In, endless supply of the Commission's report, the House of Commons passed the New South Wales Judicature Act, which set up interestingly an authoritative council.

This was not exactly yet home principle, or even agent rule, In any case it was a beginning. The Legislative Council would comprise of not more than seven, and no less than five individuals, and it served in down to earth terms just as a warning panel for the lead representative, designated by the Crown and simply engaged to discuss bills postponed by the lead representative. However, critically, assuming the lead representative proposed a law, and a straightforward greater part of the Legislative Council didn't endorse it, that law could continue no further besides on appeal to the Imperial Government.

This was unquestionably a huge development with regards to government to date, which means in reasonable terms that the powers of the lead representative were currently restricted and watched over. The Act of 1823, as it turns out, likewise presented a Supreme Court, directed by a Chief Justice.

As time advanced, the quantity of councilors situated on the lawmaking body was knock up to 15. One more significant improvement at about this time was the foundation of an autonomous press. Preceding this, the authority Sydney Gazette existed as a vehicle for the distribution of government sees, with a periodic expansion of neighborhood news.

Into this image strolled a vocation lawmaker by the name of William Charles Wentworth, who showed up in New South Wales in 1824, carrying with him a print machine. Wentworth is a fascinating person, and his name would resound through Australian legislative issues for a long time into the future. He was, indeed,

practically the quintessential frontier kid. His dad, apparently a convict, shown up on the shores of Australia on board the Neptune in 1789, arriving in Sydney with a vigorously pregnant spouse, who soon a short time later gave birth.[3]

Wentworth

William Wentworth experienced childhood in the Parramatta settlement, where his dad gained land and succeeded. Later he got back to England for his schooling, yet was back in New South Wales by 1810, and after three years, it was he who went with Gregory Blaxland and William Lawson on their pathfinding investigation of the Blue Mountains. Even later, while back in England, he concentrated on law at Cambridge and was acknowledged into the bar. He wrote the main book to be written in Australia, the awkwardly named A Statistical, *Historical, and Political Description of the Colony of New South Wales and Its Dependent Settlements in Van Diemen's Land, With a Particular Enumeration of the Advantages Which These Colonies Offer for Emigration and Their Superiority in Many Respects Over Those Possessed by the United States of America.*

Back in the province, he gained land, some freely and some acquired, and in a little while he rose to become perhaps the most well off man in New South Wales. He was, in any case, a political creature, and in any case his accomplishments in law, farming, and investigation, it is for his political work in the youthful settlement that he is best remembered.

Soon later his re-visitation of the state from his examinations abroad, the primary version of the Australian was distributed. The Australian was the main paper created in the state outside of government control. Described as an energetically basic organ of assessment, it was not extremely some time before the Australian was occupied with an angry publication crusade against the public authority, contending not least for opportunity of the press, but rather additionally for delegate government, the nullification of transportation, and preliminary by jury. He was a severe pundit of the lead representative, General Sir Ralph Darling, and the "special features" who might not give him passage into their circle upon the doubt, and the painstakingly developed gossip, that his dad was a convict.

Darling

This fight took many structures, and albeit the Australian was without a doubt adversarial on many events, frequently basically for it, its distribution in any case planted the seeds of a lively free press that would pervade broadly as the century progressed.

In 1827, Governor Darling endeavored to carry out a permitting framework to screen, expense and control what he considered a boisterous press, yet when heard by the legal executive, it was not maintained, which in itself denoted a critical development. One of the incredible problems of the early foundation of the state was to be sure the arrangement of equity and law which at first fell straightforwardly under the aegis of the lead representative's wide breadth of abilities. Unavoidable, notwithstanding, that admired English foundation, preliminary by jury, would request implantation in the

Australian settlements. Nonetheless, an extraordinary issue in a social climate overwhelmed by convicts or ex-convicts was the assurance under law that a man or lady may be attempted by a jury of friends, and under current social conditions, a free homesteader couldn't sensibly respect a convict, current or past, as a companion. At first, preliminary was normally by Judge-Advocate and six maritime or military officials, albeit later the Acts of 1823 and 1828, an individual could demand a jury if the person desired.

This issue isolated the two principle political developments in the province, the emancipists and the special features, with the previous drove by William Wentworth. Lead representative Darling for used to be not in constant conflict with Wentworth, and in reacting to strain from England, a bill was brought into the assembly and passed in 1830. It considered preliminary by jury, including jury administration by emancipists inasmuch as they had not been sentenced for a genuine crime.

It can be said, accordingly, that early constraints put on the power of the lead representative, the opportunity of the press and the execution of preliminary by jury were the initial three significant stages toward protected liberty.
However, the authoritative gathering stayed a delegated body, selected by the Crown through the workplace of the lead representative, and couldn't in this way be portrayed as agent. Full delegate government would not be executed until the cancelation of transportation, and until four new provinces had been set up in Australia.

Further Exploration

"As I stood, the main interloper on the great isolation of these verdant fields, at this point immaculate by groups and crowds, I felt aware of being the harbinger of powerful changes there." - Thomas Mitchel, explorer

Notwithstanding the tight boundaries administering the settlement of the state, courageous spirits consistently looked past the primary scope of mountains, considering what lay past. By then barely anything was known; the settled locales of the Port Jackson hinterland involved a region practically identical to Sicily according to mainland Europe, and beside the reality Mathew Flinders had affirmed that it was a landmass and not an archipelago, even the blueprint of the coast was inadequately planned and incompletely understood.

The initial test into the incredible obscure was the Blaxland-Lawson campaign, which looked to fashion an entry through the Blue Mountains, and that try deduced in the revelation of the Bathurst Plain. The process then continued with the journeys of George Bass and Mathew Flinders.

Bass

Flinders

While on his circumnavigation of the mainland, Flinders experienced a French study vessel, the Géographe, under the order of Captain Nicholas Baudin. The Géographe was in Australian waters with the information and authorization of the British specialists, and an assurance of its insurance had been given by the Admiralty, yet in any case, there was definitely doubt concerning its expectations. A supplication by its chief that the boat's central goal was simply logical was authoritatively acknowledged, notwithstanding a nearby eye was kept on it regardless. At the point when the boat got back to Europe, however, an account of its journey was distributed, presenting French classification for

geographic elements previously visited by British ships.[4] Spencer's Gulf, for instance, misleading the west of current Adelaide, became Golfe Bonaparte, and the nearby St Vincent's Gulf was renamed Golfe Joséphine. The whole area from the top of the Great Australian Bight to William's Promontory, more than 2,000 miles of shore, was named Terre Napoléon.

Remembering the tenor of relations among Britain and France right now, this could barely have been deciphered in some other manner than an outflow of French plans on setting up states on Terra Australis. There is no firm verifiable proof to help any genuine French desires to do as such, however Baudin's undertaking aroused the specialists both in England and in New South Wales to enter upon a more critical program of settlement. This was to build up a British presence all the more solidly on segments of the shoreline still for all intents and purposes open to the banner of any nation.

In 1803, under Governor Phillip King, it was concluded that the district generally helpless against French colonization was Van Diemen's Land (current Tasmania), so it was there that official consideration turned first. In September 1803, the HMS Lady Nelson, a Royal Navy study transport under Lieutenant John Bowen, arrived at a point called Risdon Cove on the River Derwent, presently part of the endless suburbia of Hobart (the momentum capital of Tasmania).
There a tactical camp was set up, yet it was moved a year after the fact to Sullivan's Cove, near the focal point of present-day Hobart. Hobarton, as it was then known, was named by the principal Lieutenant-Governor of Van Diemen's Land, Captain David Collins, to pay tribute to the then Secretary of State for War and the Colonies, Robert Hobart, fourth Earl of Buckinghamshire, the Lord Hobart.

Lord Hobart

In October 1803, it was Captain David Collins who landed almost 300 convicts at Port Phillip, near the site of present-day Melbourne, joined by a little separation of marines and a little polite staff. One of the most fascinating stories to rise out of this period of Australian settlement is that of William Buckley, a transportee from Macclesfield, Cheshire, who was indicted for having gotten a roll of fabric knowing it to have been stolen. Having shown up in Port Phillip on board the HMS Calcutta, and to a great extent left to their own gadgets on shore, Buckley and three companions got away and advanced around the inlet. While his two mates selected eventually to return and were gone forever, Buckley progressed forward, eating shellfish and berries until he was gotten to know by Aboriginals from the Watourong clan who seemed to accept that he was a rebirth of their dead clan leader. For a very long time, William Buckley lived with the Watourong, learning their language, taking an Aboriginal spouse, and fathering a few kids. In 1836, he rose up out of this life and rejoined his own general public, filling in as a mediator subsequent to getting an exoneration from the Lieutenant-Governor of Van Diemen's Land, Sir George Arthur.

An 1840 depiction of the landing at Melbourne

As destiny would have it, the Port Phillip settlement didn't keep going long, and indeed stayed in situ for under a year albeit a casual settlement stayed behind later the flight of the authority undertaking. This was the situation with a lot of early endeavors to set up settlements, and the explanation was generally in light of the fact that they were excessive other than as a highlight raise the Union Jack. Port Jackson and encompassing networks could scarcely want more space to extend, and it was for the most part perceived that the Bathurst Plain offered a practically perpetual measure of land and resources.

Therefore, when the dread of unfamiliar attack facilitated, new settlements regularly shriveled away and were abandoned.

The following settlement to be set up was Port Dalrymple, established on the north shore of Van Diemen's Land to guarantee a British presence in the Bass Strait. With a superior comprehension of the topography of the district, this was properly perceived as a significant ocean path and exchanging course the future British improvement of the locale. This campaign was shared with Lieutenant Colonel William Patterson, an official of the New South Wales Corps who showed up at the mouth of the River Tamar in November 1804, settling first at Yorktown and afterward somewhat later at Georgetown.

In October 1805, the French armada was demolished at the Battle of Trafalgar, breaking French maritime desires, yet in addition totally eliminating any danger of a French maritime endeavor against any British state anyplace. after 10 years, Napoleon would be crushed at Waterloo, and with the French repressed, India was finally taken out from any danger of a French takeover.
Spain was crumbling as an incredible magnificent power, Portugal had its hands full clutching what it had and the Dutch had stopped to involve a spot among the extraordinary exchanging countries of Europe. Subsequently, Australia was safer, so the direness to set up settlements along these lines decreased fairly. With that, the British could at their recreation affirm their royal case to the entirety of Australia.

In the 1820s, Australia remained completely neglected, however more essential focuses were recognized and involved. The settlement of Westernport occurred somewhere in the range of 1824 and 1827. Westernport, comprising of around 50 convicts, didn't keep going for long, yet Albany, comparatively settled, did get by and at last became long-lasting. The Melville Island settlement likewise did not

suffer for long yet was moved soon subsequently to the central area at Raffles Bay, the site of present-day Fort Wellington, where it turned into the premise of the city of Darwin.

In 1829, an earth shattering article of enactment was passed in the British House of Commons that announced the purview of the British lead representative general to be the whole Australian mainland. In reasonable terms, this implied that Britain made a case for Australia altogether as a magnificent belonging. No other person was in a situation to contend, and nobody did.

The cultivating of settlements, hence, proceeded at a more estimated pace, and in that year, Captain Charles Fremantle, instructing the HMS

Challenger, entered the Swan River and made a stop in one of the most amazing regular harbors on the planet. This, the site of things to come Perth, was guaranteed by Fremantle as a component of the more extensive British case to "all that piece of New Holland which is excluded inside the region of New South Wales." This, generally, implied that the western portion of the mainland would hypothetically be a settlement separate of New South Wales. New South Wales, for now, involved the whole eastern portion of the landmass, practically all of which remained totally unexplored.

Fremantle

George Pit Morison's painting of the establishing of Perth

This would not be the finish to the matter, yet meanwhile, as men were dropped in lands altogether obscure and given the essential means to make due, they normally started to test all the more profoundly inland to see what lay past the rises and bluffs. Subsequently, the vast majority of the early voyagers were simply pioneers and homesteaders occupied with breaking the ground and building up a broadly scattered arrangement of smallholdings, ranches and estates. There were surely those, chiefly later in the century, who embraced epic excursions of investigation, for the good of their own and for science, however the greater part of the guide of early Australia was drawn by pilgrims themselves, adding to the group of information in increments.

In 1815, the town of Bathurst turned into the main inland settlement in Australia, and a street was sliced across the Blue Mountains to work with it. The extent of interest presently moved to what exactly was as a result the waste arrangement of two huge waterways, the Murray and the Darling, gathered from different feeders streaming off the western inclines of the Barrier Range. These streams, while luxuriously watering the fields underneath, streamed on from that point parts obscure, and sorting out where the waters ran set off a progression of formal investigations which immediately started to bring the inside topography of the landmass into the extent of European knowledge.

The initial two critical waterways found and named on the furthest side of the Blue Mountains were both named after the lead representative, turning into the Lachlan and the Macquarie. Both of these were dependent upon fundamental investigation by
the Surveyor General of New South Wales, John Oxley. Two excursions were mounted in 1817, and for each situation, Oxley followed the waterway by boat and foot. The season was dry, in any case, and the water in the two cases scattered into wetlands prior to vanishing out and out. Regardless, albeit rather uncertain, this short series of excursions, gentle by the principles of mid nineteenth century investigation, at last uncovered what Oxley portrayed as "a nation of running waters: on each slope a spring and in each valley a stream." This was critical in light of the fact that it uncovered a scene respecting the
furrow, very much watered and of such tremendous expansiveness that it would reply to the necessities of horticultural development for generations.

Oxley

On the banks of the Brisbane River, on the east shoreline of New South

Wales, first investigated by Oxley in 1823, a province was established with the particular reason for containing convicts and detainees sentenced for additional wrongdoings during their time of punitive assistance. The waterway was additionally investigated in 1825 by Major Edmund Lockyer of the 57th Regiment of Foot, who entered to a profundity of 150 miles and got back with fresh insight about one more rich inside. All of this set up for the improvement of another settlement, and this later turned into the city of Brisbane, named to pay tribute to then legislative head of New South Wales, Major General Sir Thomas Brisbane.

Lockyer

Brisbane

A 1830s portrayal of Brisbane

The following huge endeavor to investigate the inside was driven by Hamilton Hume and William Hovell, dispatched in 1824 by Governor Brisbane.

The goal of this campaign was to investigate the domain nearby the state, and to tackle the puzzle of where the streams of western New South Wales streamed. The party voyaged southwest along the lee of the Barrier Range, crossing various streams in transit, among them the Murrumbidgee, the Murray, the Mitta-Mitta, the Owens, and the Goulburn. In the long run, they arrived at the western shore of Port Phillip at the site of the present-day city of Geelong. It is fascinating to take note of that Hume and Hovell both expected when they arrived at the coast that they were at Westernport, and they revealed back with that impact, adding that the region held great possibilities for settlement. It was on account of this that Brisbane's campaign to Westernport the next year was considered. In the event that the pioneer party had entered and settled the shores of Port Phillip, the odds are it would have stayed since conditions for horticulture and settlement positively were much better.

Simultaneously, the secret of the watershed and the progression of the streams washing the western inclines of the Barrier Range stayed unsettled. The close to take up this journey was Captain Charles Sturt, an official of the 39th Regiment of Foot who in 1828 was conceded endorsement by Governor Sir Ralph Darling to investigate the Macquarie River. Hamilton Hume joined the undertaking sometime in the future, yet aside from the disclosure and naming of the Darling River, just as the affirmation that the inside of New South Wales didn't contain an inside ocean, the campaign got back with generally little to report.

Sturt

A year later, Sturt was granted a further commission to explore Murrumbidgee River, a major tributary of the Murray River. A whaleboat was portaged over the Blue Mountains and assembled on the banks of the river before an eventful journey began. In January 1829, the Murray River was reached and named.[5] Reports of hostile encounters with Aborigines propose a hostile greeting in the inside, yet no significant episodes of brutality were recorded.

Sturt then continued down the Murray River until its confluence with the Darling River, proving that all of the rivers flowing off the western slopes found their way to the Murray River, and by following that river to its conclusion, Sturt eventually arrived at the coast. The mouth of the Murray River, scattered into a labyrinth of non-safe channels, exhausted into the sea somewhere in the range of 30 miles south of present-day Adelaide. This was fairly a disillusioning end since it created the impression that while the Murray was traversable for an extraordinary length, it was sadly not available from the ocean.

Nonetheless, Sturt's two endeavors of 1828 and 1829 are positioned as among the most significant throughout the entire existence of the mainland. In spite of the fact that there were more prominent undertakings in investigation to follow (and Sturt's own later capers were significantly more trying), the disclosure of the Darling River and the investigation of the Murray planned the main veins of a waterway framework depleting a region twofold the size of France. Maybe more significantly, the endeavor distinguished a tremendous new district ready for extremely durable British settlement.

The Henty siblings, Stephen and Edward, were vagrants in the standard Australian phrasing. They showed up in Australia in 1832, joined by their dad Thomas, a fruitful English sheep rancher from West Sussex who expected to tie down land whereupon to settle. They were allowed a huge landholding on the Swan River, on the west coast, by application to the Colonial Office, however later two periods of work, they couldn't gain any viable ground. They then explored the potential of Van Diemen's Land, but they found all available arable land there already claimed.

If there was nothing for them on Van Diemen's Land, they started to think about the contiguous central area across the Bass Strait. Various petitions were made to the British and frontier legislatures for an award of land some place inside the area, yet each time they were turned down. Eventually, they chose to settle illegally.

In December 1834, the siblings arrived on the shore of a wide inlet between present day Melbourne and Adelaide, presently known as Portland Bay, where they set up a little ranch and embraced whaling as an underlying occupation. After nine months, the adventurer and Surveyor General of New South Wales, Thomas Mitchell, coincidentally found the Henty settlement while finishing up an overview of the Darling River and was flabbergasted by what he saw. Secured in the cove was the exclusive boat, the Elizabeth, part whaler and part supply transport, and a property and nurseries. Everything was thriving, with sheep that had been brought opposite Van Diemen's Land. This unexpectedly begun an industry later on province of Victoria that would fill significantly in the future.

The Henty siblings positively stepped up to the plate, despite the fact that their establishing of a settlement and control of another quarter didn't make them numerous companions in government. The legislative leader of New South Wales, Major Sir George Gipps, wrote in a 1840 dispatch to the Secretary of State for the Colonies, Lord Russell, that regardless the case of the Henty siblings and other people who had since followed after accordingly that they had delivered a support of the Crown by establishing the settlement at their own cost, they had truth be told done nothing of the sort. The governor then proceeded to grumble fitfully at the expenses required for furnishing the settlement with the accoutrements of civilization (like a police force) and the costs of laying out a town.

Despite true protesting, the Henty siblings merged their settlement, and others went along with them. In 1851, the state of Victoria was officially settled, and in 1855, Edward Henty was chosen for the administrative get together. On schedule, the siblings were credited with building up the main settlement of Victoria, and they are additionally viewed as the authors of the fleece business in that colony.

There were numerous other unapproved settlements and family properties springing up in various areas, some more effective than others, and keeping in mind that this didn't represent a greater part of new settlements, they unquestionably contributed an incredible arrangement to the consistent dispersal of the European population.

The End of the Dream

"No EnglisH words are adequate to give a feeling of the connections between an Aboriginal gathering and its countries." - Professor W. E. H. Stanner, White Man Got No Dreaming

There has would in general be a tenacious fantasy that the Aboriginal individuals of Australia inactively looked as Europeans entered and assumed control over their territory. This may have been valid on events, however nearly from the initiation of white settlement, threats and hardships portrayed the early conflict of cultures.

In 1837, the Aborigine Protection Society was shaped in England by a little gathering of British nonconformists with an interest in guaranteeing the assurance of the sovereign legitimate and strict freedoms of local people groups falling under the Pax Britannia. This was an only a short time later the nullification of bondage in the British Empire, and this Society is regularly viewed as one of the most punctual basic liberties associations. A considerable lot of those dynamic in the Society were additionally dynamic in the nullification development of an age prior, and this checked something of an ocean change in European mentalities when it came to race and the obligation of the empire.

In 1836, as the Henty siblings and Thomas Mitchell met on the shores of Portland Bay, a British Parliamentary select advisory group was collected to research the states of native people groups in the settlements. The preface to the report of the board of trustees talks fairly to its command: "[To] think about what measures should be embraced concerning the local occupants of the nations where British settlements are made, and to the

adjoining clans, to get to them the due recognition of equity, and the assurance of their freedoms; to advance the spread of progress among them, and to lead them to the tranquil and willful gathering of the Christian religion."

This addressed every one of the major settled provinces of the domain, including India, British North America (Canada), New Zealand, South Africa, and Australia. For each situation a native populace lay in the way of European interests, and once more, in pretty much every case, the outcomes were adverse to local social orders. Some experienced more intensely than others. Indians and Africans didn't surrender with such ease to poisonous sickness as the locals of North America and Australia did, and thusly, once set free from bondage, their numbers and general flourishing improved. Nonetheless, they were as yet dependent upon greedy European monetary theft, for the most part in the capture of their property, yet additionally, in such states as Natal, in the inconsistent social limitations that kept them out of typical financial development.

The arrangement of this select board denoted a significant crossroads in British history, a second wherein the British Empire started to build up its fundamental sanction. Considering British worldwide strength, that charter necessarily included the first official acknowledgement of a responsibility inherited by the British people to balance their global ambitions with the humane usage of the aboriginal peoples falling under British sovereignty.

In many regards, this was the fundamental conundrum of the British Empire. In the post-slavery era, an enormous weight of conscience seemed to settle on the shoulders of the metropolitan population. In a by and large liberal age, the British intellectuals reacted by trying to enhance a portion of the most noticeably terrible effects of social double-dealing, particularly once the abnormally malicious impacts of European interruption into new grounds was perceived. Nonetheless, that opinion, while capably communicated and felt in England, didn't handily decipher along the boondocks, where the reasonable work of establishing a realm was occurring. The respectable savage appeared to be frequently less honorable in nearness, and the apparently crude ways of life of those like the Australian Aborigines permitted them to be interpreted as something not exactly human, and hence outside the social charter.

At the appropriate time, the frontier experts in Australia would apply various strategies of social designing that impacted the native individuals of the
alliance. In the early years, be that as it may, no such artfulness existed, and where the two societies met, and where the Aborigines opposed, they were managed both self-assertively and savagely. For instance, in Van Diemen's Land, under the governorship of Sir George Arthur, the annihilation of Aborigines was sought after with life, despite the fact that the populace was dependably little. Any components that endure the surge of illness were

wiped up later under a casual arrangement of bounty.

Again, at chances with the well known perspective on Australia's Aboriginal individuals as a detached, profound and yielding race is the way that fighting did for sure exist in their general public. Albeit barely on the size of the Maori fighting in New Zealand, or the military practices of numerous South Sea Island social orders, Aboriginal fighting appeared as fierce encounters in quest for feuds, ladies, regular assets, or neighborhood transcendence. Native weapons innovation was satisfactory for the necessities of a tracker/finder society, however scarcely the hostile hardware normally to be found in the possession of the Maoris.

It is Similarly obvious that native Australians, to a more noteworthy or lesser degree, come up short on the extent of social association important to mount anything looking like a regular conflict. The experience of outward moving Australian trailblazers and pilgrims could barely analyze, for instance, to those of the South African Boer who were matched against The Zulu and the amaNdebele, two of the best and coordinated military social orders in the non-European world. The Zulu, notwithstanding, held an unmistakable feeling of land title (though shared), and they comprehended the idea and consequences of white occupation. Ideas of Aboriginal land and land proprietorship, then again, were obscure and saturated with custom. Albeit hugely significant to them in general, vanquishing, involving and safeguarding region just didn't exist as an idea. Likewise, the social occasion of a confederation to battle a shared adversary on a considerable level was likewise essentially missing from the normal attitude. The Aborigines of Australia, subsequently, could barely have been less furnished to manage the appearance of outsiders.

Initially, in any case, the scuffle and snare strategies of the Aborigines functioned admirably. They handily paired the settlers' capacity to protect themselves with the straightforward, gag stacking dark powder weapons of the age. Things changed profoundly, in any case, right now that breech-stacking and rehashing rifles showed up on the scene. Mounted infantry and specially appointed pilgrim local armies started to

manage the paper-flimsy protections of weak Aboriginal people group. Subsequently, the overall influence started to move rapidly, and especially against the Aborigines.

What was known as the "Australian Frontier Wars" was minimal in excess of a continuous steady loss between the different sides that started very quickly and proceeded with into the twentieth century, with the last recorded

battles being logged as late as the 1930s. Intermittently the "war" erupted into recognizable fights, yet in contrast with the conflicts being battled in Africa and Asia,
nothing that happened during the "Dark Wars" ascends to whatever could be viewed as a significant clash. As a rule, they were essentially slaughters that wound up being recorded.

The primary white settlements were along the banks of the Hawkesbury River, driving inland from the waterway mouth found a couple of miles up the coast from Sydney. The district was vigorously populated by Aboriginal individuals having a place with the Darug bunch, a beach front rummaging individuals whose language included a space of around 2,300 square miles around Port Jackson and Botany Bay. What followed is presently known as the "Hawkesbury and Nepean Wars," which, from around 1795-1816, contained Aboriginal attacks on ranches and the retaliations that these incited. In 1816, Governor Macquarie conveyed a unit of the 46th Regiment of Foot to watch the populated scopes of the Hawkesbury River, finishing in a strike on a place to stay that killed 14 Aboriginals.

Similar assaults and attacks in and around Parramatta were managed by an authority authorize, made by Governor Philip King, that Aboriginals could be legitimately shot without hesitation. This was not exactly the abundance presented in Van Diemen's Land, yet it set the Aboriginals outside the security of law, disregarding the fundamental component of the British royal contract. Aside from an intermittent thunderings of worry from a far distance, no genuine exertion was made by the British government to intercede. Typically, news of an event of significance did not reach Whitehall until a year later, and another year would pass before the official reprimand was read in Sydney, at which point no one really cared anymore. Where convicts were as a rule regularly whipped nearly to death, the predicament of some unremarkable band of Aboriginals being eliminated from the land barely mixed public outrage.

The different beach front settlements experienced native individuals in almost
each example, and sometimes the contact was cordial. One model can be found in the investigations of John Oxley, who secured at Moreton Bay in 1823 returning from a visit to Port Curtis, both on the east shoreline of current Queensland. There he observed a wreck survivor who had lived among the Aborigines for quite a long time in a condition of amicability. Moreover, there is the story of William Buckley, who thrived for north of 30 years among the Aborigines.

Truth be told, models like those might have been the standard rather than the exemption had the voracious capture of land for private utilize not described each progression taken by the British as they moved further into the territory.

Nowhere was this more articulated than in Tasmania. Established as a settlement in 1803, the mild environment and richness of the island saw it foster a lively pioneer culture close by the foundation of a formal punitive state. Until the nullification of punitive transportation in 1868, Van Diemen's Land, close by Norfolk Island, filled in as the really reformatory complex, and it had become incredibly modern when the corrective framework was broken down. Simultaneously, free pioneers additionally streamed into Van Diemen's Land in consistently developing numbers, to the degree that when the Henty Brothers showed up during the 1830s, no extra arable land was accessible. In an environment such as this, the Aborigines simply had to go, and it was Governor George Arthur who pursued an extermination policy with the greatest vigor. This followed just about 25 years of weakening as native individuals, numbering something like two or three thousand regardless, not set in stone obstruction as white pioneers progressively made a case for the land. This was a stage otherwise called the "Dark War," and in its neighborhood setting, it has regularly been refered to as the best Aboriginal obstruction of the period. White fatalities numbered nearly 50 people somewhere in the range of 1828 and 1830, convincing numerous country residences to be invigorated. A shoot immediately strategy was sought after under gubernatorial announcement, and a cumbersome utilization of the death penalty saw the scaffold fill in as a significant weapon of war.

Matters reached a crucial stage in 1830 when Governor Arthur tried to achieve a finish to the continuous instability by executing a gigantic breadth across the island, known as the "Dark Line." Every physically fit male in the province joined, including convicts, and as diminishing groups of Aborigines were flushed out and killed, obstruction successfully fell. A wrecked and lessened society of native Tasmanians was assembled and

banished on Flinders Island, situated toward the upper east of Van Diemen's Land, where a booking was established under a level of government administration.

A comparable situation occurred on the Bathurst Plain when white pioneers started crossing the Blue Mountains and dividing land for the foundation of ranches. This was land involved by the Wiradjuri public, more various and more forceful overall than the Darug. Forceful Aboriginal assaults were consistently dispatched against disengaged properties, frequently joined by robbery, and these were quite often followed up by a ridiculous retaliation assault. Outskirts law won, and boondocks equity was generously applied.

In 1824, Governor Brisbane put the settled locale encompassing Bathurst under military law, for reasons, he said, "[to end] the Slaughter of Black Women and Children, and unoffending White Men." It may likewise be fascinating to take note of that it was Brisbane who set up the New South Wales Mounted Police as a paramilitary assurance power and a specialist of law enforcement. [6] The power was at first sent against bushrangers, one more wellspring of weakness on the wilderness, and an unavoidable side-effect of such a remote punitive settlement [7]

This, then, was the state of things as the colony and its various settlements slowly took root across Australia, and the dispersed aboriginal community had to digest the bitter threat that this represented to their society and way of life. As additional states were added to the advancing republic, the vicious dispossession of native individuals sped up. Matters would not be taken up by a local issues organization in any significant manner until the mid 1960s, and preceding that, ethical obligation regarding Aboriginal insurance and prosperity lay generally with Christian missionaries.

The Founding of Western Australia

"Still round the corner there may stand by another street or a second mystery gate>"
- J.R.R. Tolkien

The following meaningful step forward in the improvement of the Australian states was the foundation of Western Australia. The primary conventional settlement was Albany, and at pretty much similar time these pioneers were digging up some authentic confidence on the shores of King George's Sound, the main proper review of the Swan River was occurring under the order of Captain James Stirling on board the HMS Success. This overview was embraced in the standard Royal Navy style, joined by different specialized specialists and summed up in a brief report that contained a lot of positive analysis on the capability of the encompassing country for settlement. When that report observed its direction onto the work area of Governor Darling, plans were made to build up a super durable settlement.

The standard feelings of dread of the French setting up their shelter in a British circle of interest were expanded fairly on this event by a dread that the

Americans may do exactly the same thing. The mouth of the Swan River offered the main safe harbor on the west shore of Australia, and assuming Britain didn't effectively guarantee it, there was each motivation to assume that another person would. It is also worth bearing in mind that the almost infinite scope for growth and development in New South Wales discouraged rigorous exploration elsewhere, so as far as the British government was concerned, dumping a handful of convicts on the site and hoisting the Union Jack would, for the time being at least, be enough to stake a legal British claim.

There was, notwithstanding, a force social occasion of Private capital participating in intermediary magnificent undertakings, as confirmed by the tremendous impact of the Hudson Bay Company and the British East India Company. Both controlled huge districts with virtual restraining infrastructures on each accessible asset and very little in the method of direct majestic control. By then, the Australian Agricultural Company, with a starting capital of £1,000,000, was active in New South Wales, and the Van Diemen's Land Company operated in that colony. Private capital, along these lines, ended up very inspired by the possibilities of Western Australia.

One of the principal Britons to show such interest was Thomas Peel, the cousin of future Prime Minister Sir Robert Peel. Strip offered the public authority a plan to settle 10,000 pioneers at £30 per head in return for an award of 4,000,000 sections of land of land. Accordingly, the public authority jeered, and Peel was guided out the entryway, however he stayed courageous. All things considered, he chose to continue with his own assets, and upon a venture of £50,000, a monster aggregate back then, he set forth for Western Australia abroad The Parmelia, showing up on June 1, 1829 with 50 pilgrims. The *Parmelia*, it just so happens, was captained by James Stirling, and it was he who risked upon the ideal site for the foundation of a town. Perth, he later wrote,
"[is] as lovely as anything of this sort I had at any point seen." They therefore established the Swan River Colony.

As the principal pioneers battled to set up a foothold, more were convinced by Peel's representatives, and by January 1830, 25 boats had handled approximately 850 free pilgrims. A populace of 1,300 was apportioned 525,000 sections of land of land, and during 1830, a further 1,000 men, ladies, and kids were landed. Quite expeditiously, the essentials of an energetic British settlement were established.

The early homesteaders in Western Australia endured harsh and hard encounters. In 1830, for instance, there were 4,000 people enlisted as inhabitants in the settlement, yet after two years that figure had dropped to just 1,300. Strip lost nearly everything, and the early settlement was depicted as "the scarecrow of human progress." However, even as many crushed individuals went to England, others remained, and in spite of the difficulties, the Swan River Settlement survived.

The occupants had no clue there were incredible stores of gold covered in Australian soil there, so the settlement stayed farming in nature. It before long became evident, notwithstanding, that this was not the sort of country that could uphold laborer ranchers of minor property. Regardless, this region required enormous scope landowners to carry out stock raising on a critical scale, and this would ultimately occur. By 1840, the populace had recuperated, numbering above 5,000.

There was at first an assurance to keep convicts out of this settlement, In any case work was scant, and as adaption to enormous parcels of land proceeded, work in expanding amounts was required. Under the governorship of Charles Fitzgerald, a speculative program of convict importation started, formalized by a request in gathering of the British Parliament sanctioned on May 12, 1849. This brought about the importation of nearly 10,000 convicts, and Perth as a result turned into a correctional state. However, an adjusting number of sponsored free pilgrims were consistently presented by the British government, to a great extent as a settlement measure against profound uneasiness at the presentation of such countless convicts. The benefit lay now in the accessibility of work for the development of streets and general framework, and the capacity to foster the manor economy of the settlement. It was not well before Perth took root.

Once their sentences were served, a considerable lot of these men floated away to different states and different areas of the world, driving Fitzgerald to comment that "Western Australia is, truth be told, a simple course pipe through which the ethical sewage of Great Britain is poured upon those networks." However, because of the foundation and perseverance of the Swan River Colony, Western Australia did without a doubt presently lie solidly inside the British authoritative reach. The test in financed migration, coordinated and methodical, had worked, and this provoked further interest in efficient colonization. Accordingly, those in power, both in Britain and in the developing Australian settlements, started to consider extending the program to incorporate the leftover agitated locales of the huge land on the continent.

South Australia and Tasmania

"In reporting to the Colonists of His Majesty's Province of South Australia the foundation of the Government, I thus call upon them to act consistently with request and quietness, appropriately to regard the laws, and by a course of industry and temperance, by the act of sound profound quality, and a severe recognition of the laws of religion, to substantiate themselves to be qualified to be the Founders of an extraordinary and free Colony." - Captain Sir John Hindmarsh, the primary legislative head of South Australia

One of the implications of the Industrial Revolution was the ascent of a class of metropolitan poor. Low wages, scant work, the decrease of cabin enterprises, and the development of metropolitan ghettos were indications of this new time, and it prompted England being overpopulated during a period that the British Empire controlled huge and void areas from one side of the planet to the other. Migration was viewed as an undeniable arrangement, yet Thomas Peel had experienced a monetary calamity with his Swan River analysis, and there were not many able to attempt that strategy again.

However, in 1829, an elective idea of colonization was recommended in a book entitled A Letter from Sydney. This book was composed by Edward Gibbon Wakefield, a generally average man who had never left the shores of England yet by and by introduced a novel thought. Strip had introduced his plan on a wealth of modest land, yet Wakefield pushed something altogether unique, recommending that the specialists sell land in the states at a reasonable market cost. His reasoning was just that for a settlement to be fruitful, land, capital, and work were totally required. Cheap

land would draw in the yeomanry to homesteading, denying the enormous landowner with strong capital the work that he wanted. Capital speculation would not be drawn to a province without work, and there were states in what might these days be the creating scene that offered colossal pools of native work. Clearly, a manor economy had a superior shot at making headway in any of them.

Thus, Wakefield recommended the foundation of an asset to actuate white work from England to dare to the provinces. Installment for work would be determined to guarantee that following a few years of work, an individual who headed abroad would have adequately saved to purchase his own territory. This would likewise serve to sift through the globe-trotters who every now and again took up land and deserted it soon subsequently. The offer of land would support the expenses of immigration.

Wakefield framed a colonization society, and it was fused at practically exactly the same time Charles Sturt presented his overview of the Murray

River catchment to the workplace of the lead representative. In it he uncovered the presence of a huge hold of arable land, and this helpful occurrence of conditions prompted the arrangement of the settlement of South Australia.

In 1831, the South Australia Land Company was framed, In any case Wakefield found the British government inquisitively shy about approving the exchange of sway to a privately owned business, despite the fact that it had not many doubts about doing that somewhere else. An affiliation was shaped all things considered, the South Australian Association, which maybe felt less in an exposed fashion business than an organization, and under the condition that the new settlement be administered straightforwardly from Whitehall through a lead representative, another state was approved. However, while the British government may in fact control, the offer of land would be directed by a leading group of magistrates containing the primary financial backers in the plan, so a private office really called the shots. This would arise at the appointed time as the South Australia Company, established on a capital membership of
£200,000. Eventually, the British government did it for barely anything, as it so regularly did, by permitting private funding to spearhead the settlement and take care of the bills, while simultaneously guaranteeing sway over any new domain founded.

The lead representative named by the Colonial Office to run South Australia was Royal Navy Captain Sir John Hindmarsh. The underlying corps of pioneers would be dropped on Kangaroo Island, lying a couple of miles seaward of Cape Jarvis,
near advanced Adelaide. The settlement was before long continued on to the central area, in any case, and the site of Adelaide was chosen as the future capital.

Hindmarsh

A 1839 portrayal of Adelaide

Van Diemen's Land had kept on existing as a reliance of New South Wales, serving the capacity of a punitive settlement, however in 1825, through a demonstration passed by Parliament, the two domains were isolated and the foundations of a different pioneer government were set up. As a correctional province, and under the governorship of Sir George Arthur, a man completely like Bligh when it came to dictatorial inclinations, Van Diemen's Land turned into the home of frantic men and hard cases, and the system was reasonably unforgiving and solid. Arthur likewise turned out to be the one who put a last finish to Aboriginal opposition, which, joined with the details of correctional help on the island, stepped him and his province with a famous reputation.

Thanks to these exercises, by the last part of the 1830s, Australia comprised of the states of New South Wales, Van Diemen's Land (the main settlement with characterized borders), Western Australia, and Southern Australia. Victoria, Queensland, and the Northern Territories still needed to be set up. Victoria would be the following piece of the riddle set up, however this would not come until one of the most significant occasions of early Australian history: the revelation of gold.

The End of the Convict Era

"25 lAshEs under my observation had similar impact as 1,000 lashes under some other individual's hand." – Mr. E.A. Slad, from the report of the Select Committee

If one was to underscore any episode of early Australian history, it would be the cancelation of corrective transportation to the landmass, a training that had characterized the realm's first provincial experiences in Australia.

The start of the finish of coordinated correctional transportation accompanied the audit of a parliamentary select board attempted somewhere in the range of 1837 and 1838. Under the heaviness of two considerable reports, the fundamental end was that transportation didn't discourage wrongdoing, however it spoiled the social nature of the states. This therefore prompted a commission of request, the Molesworth Commission.

Much of the catalyst for both of these was crafted by an early corrective reformer and common liberties advocate by the name of Alexander Maconochie.

Maconochie was a tall and rather grave man, a Royal Navy commander and an establishing individual from the Royal Society who acknowledged the place of private secretary to Governor Sir John Franklin. Maconochie was, in actuality, a covert operative, embedded by the liberal helpful development in Britain to report back in a decent way on conditions for convicts on the island.

His report, when at last total, made a huge mix both in England and in Van Diemen's Land, the previous as a result of the vile conditions depicted and the last on the grounds that an unwanted light was out of nowhere radiating on rehearses since quite a while ago kept stowed away. The episode added to the review of Governor John Franklin and set off an overall parliamentary survey. It is additionally reasonable for note that an overall development towards liberal compassion was happening back home, so the obsolete British punitive code was ready for survey and correction. The incredible jail reformer Elizabeth Fry drove a development of invested individuals, inside which Maconochie was the undisputed specialized master, and this development recognized the chronologically misguided nature of the whole custom of transportation.

Fry

The parliamentary select board took a lot Of declaration from compelling sources inside the state, where a solid development additionally existed for the training to end. For this situation it had less to do with compassionate worries and more to do with the unreasonable rivalry made by free work. Of course, homesteaders in Australia additionally stressed over common security worries that emerge in a general public so overwhelmed by criminal elements.

To put it plainly, correctional transportation had run its course, and it was presently just an issue of destroying it as fast as British parliamentary techniques would permit. Maconochie's harsh report provoked a quick modification of jail conditions in lieu of nullification; up to 1836, the framework had presented a round figure of 100,000 convicts to Australia, and on that date nearly 45,000 remained confined under different terms in a few locations.

Most of these were normal lawbreakers, alongside incidental political detainees and a modest bunch of what were curiously known as "refined men convicts."

Transportation to New South Wales finished in 1840, however offices on Norfolk Island and Van Diemen's Land stayed functional, with managerial obligation regarding the previous moving at last to Hobart. Van Diemen's Land stayed the main working reformatory province, including Norfolk Island, which was held as a repository for the hardest cases and those indicted for extra wrongdoings during their terms of transportation.

The continuous transportation of convicts to Van Diemen's Land was gone against by various nearby social orders and associations, including the Australasian Anti-Transportation League, different metro and church gatherings, and various associations and bodies in the United Kingdom itself. The training was suspended momentarily in 1846, however it was immediately restored when prompt congestion in British metropolitan jails started to be felt. By then, terms of imprisonment had in any case been redefined, and convicts were now termed "exiles." Since the whole framework was presently under reliable survey, the most exceedingly awful abundances of treatment and conditions had facilitated considerably.

The last convict transport dispatched from England to Van Diemen's Land, the St Vincent, showed up in 1853, and the last boat to depart England, the Hougoumont, left in 1867 and showed up in Western Australia on January 10, 1868. Among the early states, South Australia was the one in particular that never acknowledged convicts from Britain, yet it acknowledged convicts from inside the region.

Pair with the finish of the convict framework, British settlement turned out to be all the more outright. The down to earth obtaining and dispersion of land had always

been aimless, impromptu, and generally unregulated, and it set aside a lot of effort for the British government to accept the certainty that, having gotten the cycle under way, sway over the whole landmass would just involve time. The public authority, in this manner, appeared consistently to be a few stages behind current realities on the ground. This likewise was helped by the huge distances included, the totalitarian powers allowed early lead representatives, and the various styles of government that each worked. Land was taken care of by different lead representatives altogether as per their own impulses and tendencies, and this inclination proceeded until 1831, when better control of the interaction was expected by Whitehall, which proclaimed from there on that land must be settled by auction.

Passage through the Blue Mountains and the land surge that followed pulled in enormous capital. The Australian Agricultural Company, joined by Royal Charter, was formalized by a parliamentary demonstration in 1824. Part of the command of the organization was "for the development and improvement of waste terrains in the state of New South Wales." A parcel of land estimating 500,000 sections of land was made accessible for no installment. Similarly, the Van Diemen's Land Company, additionally fused under a Royal Charter, gotten 400,000 sections of land for a yearly rental of £468.

This can be viewed as an authentic designation of land, essentially as indicated by the guidelines and guidelines conceived by the public authority. At the opposite finish of the range lived any semblance of the Henty siblings and the "vagrants." The term vagrant, as it was applied to land occupation in Australia, was gotten from a comparative term utilized in America that portrayed people or gatherings involving land without legitimate title. In the good 'ol days, this basically came concerning when a convict, having served out his term, recognized a piece of unused ground, assembled a shanty, and started farming and development. Typically this was joined by smuggling, bushranging, and different violations, all of which gave vagrants a poor reputation.

The expansion of crouching, particularly once the land past the Blue Mountains had been opened up, came about altogether on the grounds that there were scarcely any perceived guidelines. It was consistently inconsequential to attempt to prevent individuals from extending outwards, and without a trace of method for making a case for title, hunching down was inescapable. It is likewise a fact that land was a boundless asset around then, so there appeared to be no good reason for squandering managerial assets managing crouching when such a lot of land was accessible for anyone who needed it. Meanwhile, the huge landowners created crops in amount and the aggregation of vagrant creation started to contribute a lot to the expense base and the developing economy. In the long run, authoritizes managed vagrant land by giving touching licenses and different grants for an ostensible yearly stipend.

By 1835, the pioneer organization branches started to consider the legitimateness of land awards gave during the time of oppressive lead representatives, and this momentarily shook the financial establishments of the different settlements. At the point when counseled, the law officials gave it as their viewpoint that each discretionary award of land from the date of the establishment of New South Wales were invalid.
The next year, notwithstanding, a demonstration of parliament immediately

regularized these, "… to eliminate such questions and to calm the titles of His Majesty's subjects holding or qualified for hold any land in New South Wales."

Under Governor George Gipps (1837-1846), a guideline was placed into impact that permitted, by extraordinary review, anybody keeping £5,120 to obtain great many sections of land of land any place they picked. Before the indiscretion of this was acknowledged, eight such cases had been made and formalized, all nearby towns. This was a theoretical endeavor with respect to a few well off men, and they procured galactic benefits inside a couple of years, particularly when metropolitan land costs jumped in esteem in the repercussions of the gold rush.

Gipps

In the end, the utilization of the expression "vagrant" developed from limited scope scoundrel homesteaders to suggest enormous scope landowners or tenants who ran huge